OLOGY

WITHDRAWN

the *best* in
swimwear
design

Joy McKenzie

B.T. Batsford Ltd • London

◀ **Gottex:** 'Casino' bandeau one-piece swimsuit
with detachable straps and matching pareo, from
a mixture of nylon and Lycra.

Acknowledgements

I would like to thank my family and friends, and those most directly involved in the production of this publication without whose support it would not have been possible. To Richard Reynolds, Executive Editor and Martina Stansbie, Editor at B.T. Batsford Ltd; Liz Earle, GMTV's Health & Beauty presenter and author of the best-selling *Bikini Diet* books; Carol Spencer, author of *Style Counsel*; Peter G. Yarranton, Chairman of the Sports Council; Mark McCormack, international sports promoter; Paul Hammond and Monica Fernandez of R.D. Franks Ltd; Dominic Hilton-Foster, Press Officer at Harrods; the London College of Fashion Library; the National Art Library; the British Fashion Council; the Amateur Swimming Association; Caroline Carr at the Women's Sports Foundation; Helen Bonsor at the British Sports and Allied Industries Federation; and the British Sports Council.

Dedication

This book is dedicated to my parents Mitchell and Monica McKenzie.

© Joy McKenzie 1998

First published 1998

Printed in Singapore by Kyodo Printing Co.

for the Publisher

B.T. Batsford Ltd

583 Fulham Road

London SW6 5BY

http://www.batsford.com

ISBN 0 7134 8039 4

A CIP catalogue record for this book is available from the British Library.

contents

Introduction   6

The One-Piece Swimsuit   22

The Two-Piece Swimsuit   74

Cover-Ups   114

Accessories   122

Index   126

Introduction

One Piece or Two?

Swimwear can be divided into two categories: one-piece and two-piece swimsuits. The one-piece swimsuit, formerly known as a 'bathing suit', has the longer history. Bathing dress for the two sexes developed at different paces, and was indicative of differing attitudes. Men generally swam in the nude, up into the middle of the nineteenth century. Very few women actually swam: the female bather was passive, unlikely to immerse herself in the water. In, say, 1865, she was more likely to be found walking beside the shore in a bathing costume consisting of a tunic and overshirt, usually in a woven serge or wool fabric, with ankle-length bloomers or knickers made from wool. Swimming was practically impossible in this clothing. The bathing suit also had design details, such as overskirts, blouses and lace or embroidered trimmings.

The one-piece swimsuit exemplified the liberation of women in the late nineteenth century, as they became able to bicycle and bathe and required the appropriate clothes for such activities. In around 1880, the cumbersome tunic and knickers were replaced by a top and pants (sometimes with an attached skirt). This was suitable for women and children, and was popularized by the swimmer Annette Kellerman. Competitive swimming became an accepted sport. As a result, American scientific hygienists approved the combination of water and exercise in the 1920s, and so modern swimwear was born. Its subsequent development was rapid and extensive.

The two-piece swimsuit, more commonly known as the bikini, first appeared in the 1920s, featuring a high front and back (although a late Roman mosaic of AD 406 depicts several ladies wearing an identical garment). The style was considered a little too daring, and it was modified to include a skirt. Changes to the cut of the neckline and back resulted in this style becoming the standard female costume for the next decade and a half. The true bikini did not appear until the mid-1940s, consisting of a bra-like top and pants. It caused a sensation on the beaches in France and the USA, and did not find general acceptance until the 1960s and 1970s. The bikini is not

▶ **Slix:** 'The Corsetry Connection' – a 1940s swimsuit.

practical for competitive swimming, but is suitable for leisure activities such as sun-bathing and is even available in specially-designed 'tan-through' fabrics.

The present-day female competitive swimsuit is a form-fitting, skirtless, high-front 'racer-back' suit, manufactured in the latest fabrics, incorporating streamlining features: the result of much research. When the excellent printing and dyeing properties of nylon were recognized, fashion – in the guise of stripes and prints – was introduced into competitive swimwear; each season saw a new release of prints and colours. The relationship between fashion and swimwear design continues today.

For anyone who feels self-conscious or lacks confidence in their figure, the one-piece swimsuit is the better choice. It is a fashionable alternative that accounts for 60 per cent of all swimsuit sales. A compromise style would be a bikini with a cover-up, such as a T-shirt or a sarong.

Men, in the meantime, were effecting their own modifications in the interest of speed. In the late 1930s, the men's full-length one-piece costume gave way to the hip-high, half-skirted trunk. However, the top male swimmers of the early 1950s preferred to wear their cotton costumes inside out, so that the garment appeared skirtless (the skirt hidden inside). Soon the skirtless version of the men's racing costume appeared in competition, originally made in silk.

Other design changes during the past twenty years have been less in magnitude, but still significant for competitive swimmers. First, the outer skirt was replaced by an inner lining, reducing drag. Next, the cut of the trunk was abbreviated, so that it sat lower on the hips: this was the direct forerunner of today's racing brief.

Costume Styling

Swimsuits, both one- and two-piece, can be found in a variety of styles, shapes, cuts, colours and patterns. Today the silhouette (overall shape) is perhaps the most important factor in swimwear design. Only the best fabrics are considered, after

▶ **Fürstenberg:** one-piece swimsuit from 80 per cent polyamide and 20 per cent Lycra. Photograph: Lycra only by DuPont.

rigorous selection and testing of the fabric 'bases'. A new silhouette is designed and cut using Computer Aided Design and Computer Aided Manufacture (CAD/CAM) systems. Garments are usually modelled on a live model to ensure an accurate fit. A new silhouette may be amended and fitted as many as five times. Once the fit is approved, the garment is 'swim trailed' – virtually to destruction. After the basic design has been finalized, all the other fittings and sizes are manufactured.

There is a choice between a high- or low-cut leg. A high-cut leg will give the appearance of a longer leg, but attention should be paid to the pattern, which can draw attention to the hip area. The low-cut leg is more popular, and certainly more conservative, giving a longer body effect and a 1950s glamour style. The 'boy line' leg, or 'boy shorts', is a two-piece swimsuit designed with shorts, which may be cuffed, that come down to the top of the thigh. This is a style that flatters the athletic body.

Underwired swimsuits, together with padded and moulded cups, certainly make the most of a woman's cleavage, as well as providing support. Many swimsuits are available with push-up wires and padding, the latter sometimes removable. Following the huge success of the Wonderbra, the trend continues towards underwired and padded swimwear. An underwired swimsuit is very versatile, and can be worn as a body in the daytime, and during the evening with matching co-ordinates such as wraps, skirts and trousers.

For a sporty look, support and structure are given by panelling the swimsuit, although it may be underwired too. The use of panels can serve to enhance the curves on a flatter figure, especially if the panels are in a patterned material against a darker, plain-coloured background. They can also offer additional support. This links corsetry and lingerie with swimwear, both in styling and by making a woman's figure appear slimmer.

The more detail to seams or panels the swimsuit has, the more flexible and versatile it will be, for example as a top with a skirt or with a pair of beach shorts. Seams around the bosom and material gathered in at the centre can enhance and support without the rigidity of underwiring. A style that covers the whole of the chest

▶ **Huit:** 'Tulip' one-piece swimsuit from 80 per cent polyamide and 20 per cent elastane.

up to the neck is also stylish, and popular with women who have had a mastectomy or other breast operations.

There are plenty of 'sporty' styles to choose from, mainly in black or white, or stripy combinations of the two. These suits contain a high Lycra content, featuring design details such as wide shoulder straps, tank-style tops and high-waisted, shorts-styled bottoms. One-piece suits of different cuts and colours can be worn over each other for extra support and to achieve a fashionable layered look. The sporty look is clearly evident in the cropped tops. Such tops are more concealing and supportive for all forms of exercise, not exclusively swimming..

A feminine look – but strictly for the ultra-thin who require no bra support at all – can be achieved with 'spaghetti-strap' swimsuits. Bikini versions are also available, with matching string effects at hip level. These styles have returned with the emergence of the 1990s' Glam look. The strapless top is still a favourite for sun-bathing, and some designs have optional halter-neck straps: reassuring when swimming.

In contemporary swimwear design, the trend is towards glossy Lycra. Wet-look range cotton Lycras are still very popular for those prefer a natural fibre next to their skin. Seersucker is also a popular choice. It should be noted that shiny fabrics reflect light and thus seem to increase the wearer's size in areas such as stomach, bottom and breasts. If a woman is above-average in size, then matt cotton fabrics are recommended.

Swimwear Fabrics

There have been many developments in swimwear fabrics in recent years. Innovations such as the new Sun Select fabric from Triumph even allow tanning through the swimsuit; it has been designed to block harmful UVB rays, allowing only the safer UVA rays to penetrate to the skin. Speedo's Scubasuit is made in a dense fabric which has a sun protection factor (SPF) of over 30, dry or wet, to help the wearer practise 'safe

▶ **Arena:** one-piece swimsuit from 80 per cent polyamide and 20 per cent Lycra. Photograph: Lycra only by DuPont.

sun'. Triumph have also developed a material which is quick-drying, handy for swimming holidays. It is a mixture of nylon and Lycra with a layer of Teflon, meaning water rolls off the surface of the suit.

Speedo is one of the largest manufacturers of swimwear, and is at the forefront of hi-tech fabric development. The company has produced a range of fabrics to meet various budgets and uses. Because all elastane fibres degrade in chlorine, Speedo use Lycra elastane fibre in their fabrics. Although this is considered the most chlorine-resistant of fabrics, a regular or competitive swimmer may require a suit of 100 per cent polyester for training. For men's swimwear, only 100 per cent Polyamide Tricot Warp Knit is used. Speedo's 100 per cent polyamide swimwear is manufactured from bright Tricobal yarn, within a warp-knitted construction. The fabric is durable and has sound resistance to snagging, abrasion and chemical attack, while providing generous width extension to ensure a smart, comfortable fit. This fabric is therefore suitable for training, school use and general day-to-day requirements.

Polyester ultra-stretch fabric can be used for men's, women's and children's swimsuits. It is a warp-knitted fabric, usually produced in bright polyester, employing textured and flat yarns, with a unique construction to import high-quality extension properties. This is a durable, chemical-resistant fabric with excellent colour-fastness. Like the 100 per cent Polyamide Tricot Warp Knit, it is ideal for training, school use, and everyday swimming.

100 per cent Polyester Weft knit is a weft-knitted interlock-based fabric knitted from bright, textured, polyester yarns. It is durable and specifically developed for improved resistance to abrasion, pulling and snagging, and to reduce the incidence of white-fibre migration on transfer-printed designs. This double-faced fabric also gives added comfort. Polyamide/Lycra Elastane Woven Fabric, used to make 'Paper suits', is a lightweight woven fabric with Lycra. The paper-like material is favoured by competition swimmers because it provides the ultimate in hydrodynamics.

Polyamide/Lycra Elastine Tricot Fabric is used in most competitors' swimsuits, as the

▶ **Björn Borg:** sport top and sport Thai. The red zip front bikini is made from 91 per cent polyamide and 9 per cent elastane.

competitive swimming environment presents unusual hazards to fibres and fabrics. Prolonged exposure to chlorinated water, excessive perspiration, extensive variable tension due to the swimmer's body movements, and, in many cases, exposure to bright sunshine have an adverse effect on fabric performance. This combination of hazards presents a peculiar problem to the industry and demands special fibres. To give satisfactory performance, DuPont have developed variations on the brand leader in elastane fibres, Lycra.

Lycra, when woven in blends with polyamide and polyester, gives swimwear fabrics stretch and recovery, to produce a high-quality fabric giving the garment 'second-skin' fit; these characteristics are not matched by polyamide fabrics. The fabric's performance can, however, be affected by the particularly adverse conditions of competitive swimming, mentioned above. For this purpose, DuPont have developed an elastane fibre, Lycra type 239B, for immersion in chlorinated water, particularly when this immersion combines with human perspiration. The Lycra has been produced to reduce degradation when subjected to the particular conditions of, and is therefore most effective when used in, competitive swimming. Lycra type 239B uses DuPont's elastane, and is recommended for use only when demands on fabric performance become unusually critical.

P.B.T. Endurance is a fabric exclusive to Speedo, and consists of a blend of 45 per cent polyester and 55 per cent P.B.T. – a polyester variant. The resulting warp-knitted fabric has superior stretch and recovering properties. It is durable, does not degrade and, because of the polyester base, colour resistance to sand and chlorinated water, is superior to polyamide fabrics. A lower water absorption rate enables a quick drying time; the lightweight finish gives improved resistance to drag factors. This fabric is ideal for training purposes, club and school use and everyday swimming.

DuPont also produces Supplex, used particularly in aquatic fitness-training exercise

▶ **Maru:** 'Skooba' training suit with a high neck (neck clip) from 80 per cent nylon and 20 cent Lycra; it is soft and sticky to the touch, lightweight, fast-drying and offers resistance to chlorine.

clothing. Supplex is made from a nylon/Lycra combination which feels like cotton. Its main benefit is that it is hard-wearing, and therefore has high resistance to repetitive washing. It dries extremely quickly. In short, it is ideal for garments that will be used regularly and extensively.

In the 1920s, swimsuits were manufactured in pure silk, for lightness, while racing and training costumes were made from cotton. Navy blue was the only colour option. Silk was more costly than cotton, but it had several advantages: lightness, strength, elasticity and feel, which were behind its dominance in swimwear for the leading competitive swimmers.

Extensive use of silk and cotton continued through the 1930s and 1940s. Competitive swimming was naturally curtailed during the Second World War. Until and including the 1956 Olympic Games in Melbourne, silk and cotton were the leading swimwear fabrics. In the Melbourne Olympics the top racing swimsuits were made from silk with cotton. In 1957, Australian swimmer Dawn Fraser developed a new competitive swimsuit for Speedo – in the new wonder fabric: nylon.

Of the synthetics, nylon was the most favoured because of its strength, elasticity and the ease with which it took colour when dyed. Nylon was particularly suitable as a swimwear fabric because it was lightweight. Its appeal was heightened by its water-repellent quality, which also meant that it was quick-drying. With the introduction of nylon, colours other than navy began to appear in the competition pool: red and royal blue were the most popular.

The 1972 Munich Olympic Games proved a launching pad for Lycra, the last of the major synthetic fibres to find its way into competitive swimwear. It has excellent stretch properties as well as good recovery and lightness. The durability of this elastomeric fibre was not on a par with nylon, and the higher initial fabric cost soon ensured that the new suits were set aside for competition, rather than all-purpose wear, in which nylon remained dominant.

▶ **Amaya Arzuaga:** bikini.
Photograph: Outumuro

Lycra became more prominent with the rise of the East German swimmers, especially the young women who took part in the Belgrade World Championships in 1973. It is debatable as to whether they received competitive benefit from their new two-way stretch, form-fitting swimsuits; collectively, they did swim better than their opposition, and one of the things that distinguished them from their competitors was their swimsuits.

Today the quest for new swimwear fabric continues. Manufacturers expend much time and money on research. Swimmers, too, are constantly seeking to employ the latest technology to keep up with, but preferably ahead of, the opposition.

Triumph International

▶ **Triumph International**

The One-Piece Swimsuit

Since the 1920s, the majority of bathing suits have been designed for beach wear rather than swimming. Between the 1920s and the 1940s, bathing suits were made of knitted fabrics, usually wool jersey. The first rib-knit elasticated one-piece bathing suit was produced in the USA by the Jantzen Company in the 1920s. Designers such as Chanel were instrumental in promoting bathing suits, and Jean Patou introduced bathing suits with cubist inspired designs.

Within a decade, fabrics gained elasticity, and exhibitionism of all kinds – particularly from movie stars – set in. Medical approval of the sun and trends in fitness and exercise combined and ideal swimwear ceased to be 'undressed dress' and became modest nudity.

The maillot was the classic one-piece knitted, or jersey, swimsuit without skirt, form-fitting and usually backless. Sometimes it had detachable straps that could be tied around the neck or buttoned to the back of the suit.

During the 1940s, bathing suits could hardly be considered essential items of clothing. The classic swimsuit of the time was known as the dressmaker's suit: it was made from knitted or woven fabric, styled with a skirt, and sometimes shirred across the back with elastic thread. The invention of fast-drying lightweight fabrics helped to popularize swimming. The late 1940s saw swimwear styles in aqua satin, with all-over ruched backs, gathering down the centre front and halter-neck ties.

In the 1950s, the bathing suit or costume became known as a swimsuit. With the revolt against austerity, women tried to find styles that would enhance their femininity. It was the era of constructed or sculptured suits which emphasized the bust and minimized the waist, echoing the foundation garments of the time: swimsuits were often boned and corseted. Two of the most popular styles of the time were the star daisy romper and the shirred panel suit. Fabrics began to riot with colours and prints. Inspiration came from the cinema, starting with halter styles and ending with strapless. Marilyn Monroe exploited the bathing suit as 'an essential weapon in her promotion.'

▶ **Rasurel:** turquoise/green one-piece swimsuit from a nylon/Lycra mixture.

During the 1960s, foreign travel became more common. Manufacturers produced clothes that would give a wardrobe the maximum effectiveness in the minimum of space: packable and uncrushable. Israeli Bennett Fashions, such as patterned swimsuits with matching long skirts, became popular. The bloomer suit was also popular at this time, made in a romper style with bouffant pants gathered into elastic bands at the legs. Briefer swimsuits appeared, cut away around the tops of the thighs and around the arms and shoulders, exemplified in the cut-out suit, which was introduced in the mid-1960s. This was a fitted maillot swimsuit with sections cut out at the sides, at the centre front, or indeed anywhere; occasionally fishnet was inserted into the cut-outs, or laces connected the cut-out sections.

Men's trunks in this period had thigh-length legs and elasticated waistband, and were frequently styled with three contrasting stripes down the side. During the decade, swimsuits continued to get briefer and briefer, a trend that continued into the next decade.

In the 1970s swimwear fashion became associated with beauty contests. There was a passion for gold, turbans and ethnic fashion. However there was also an emphasis on practical swimwear, especially important in competitive swimming. Olympic swimmers felt better in one-piece swimsuits such as the skin suit, primarily designed for competitive swimming, and first seen in the 1972 Munich Olympic Games. These suits were manufactured from very fine cotton that became virtually transparent when wet. It was rumoured that these suits might have been banned had it not been for the outstanding performance of the East German women's swimming team who wore them. The skin suit underwent further development, and its subsequent incarnation was made from a thin, lightweight Lycra/nylon mixture, more revealing than its predecessor, which would cling closely to the body and thereby reduce drag.

Reducing drag for competitive swimming has been a preoccupation for designers, manufacturers and swimmers alike. The Swiss Olympic swimmers of 1972 decided to wear suits which were glued around the neck, leg and arm openings, which prevented water and air bubbles from entering the suits. Removing the glue was extremely

▶ **Margaret Howell:** one-piece swimsuits with scooped necklines and skirted bottoms, reminiscent of the 1940s, made from a mixture of cotton and nylon.

painful, however: that solution was not used again. Soon other teams were taking advantage of the skin suit, produced by two manufacturers in particular, Arena and Speedo. Arena's swimsuits were seen in the French Swimming Championships at Vitel in 1973, and during the Montreal Olympics, worn by the American, British, Russian, Brazilian and Spanish teams. The major advantage was that the body was completely compressed by the suit. The embarrassment caused by the suit's transparency was reduced by the use of highly coloured patterns. In light of the problems associated with competitive swimwear, it seemed at one time that the only alternative would be to swim naked. Flat-chested women might actually swim faster, under these conditions, and in fact this was an option offered to competitors in the 1980 Moscow Olympics.

In the 1980s, swimsuits were sculptured around the lines of the body and were cut to come higher at the sides, revealing virtually all of the leg. As the trend to wear less clothing altogether has prevailed, Jantzen revealed their no-suit swimsuit.

Contemporary swimsuits are no-nonsense, streamlined and sporty. The innovations of fabric technology has completely revolutionized the swimwear market. One example is Speedo's Aquablade swimsuit worn by the Irish 1996 Atlanta Olympic gold medallist, Michelle Smith. After the Olympics, Aquablade sales broke all records: 100,000 sold in Japan and 25,000 in Europe. Swimsuits like these undergo at least 40 different tests before they are considered fit to be worn. These include resistance to sea-water, light, chlorine, washing, snagging, strength, stretch, pilling, transparency, porosity and friction.

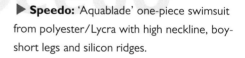

▶ **Speedo:** 'Aquablade' one-piece swimsuit from polyester/Lycra with high neckline, boy-short legs and silicon ridges.

▲ **Gottex:** 'Best' one-piece navy swimsuit with white and navy rope effect rim and sheer navy insets down the sides. Made from nylon with Lycra.

▲ **S/G by Gottex:** 'Zet' black-and-white zebra print suit with cut out sides and ring centre bra. Made from nylon and Lycra.

Gottex

▲ **Triumph International:** 'Amourette 64041' flamingo velour one-piece swimsuit with seaming and wide shoulders from 75 per cent acetate, 15 per cent polyamide and 15 per cent Lycra elastane.

◀ **Triumph International:** 'Amourette 64021' white one-piece swimsuit with horizontal stitch detail. The 85 per cent polyamide and 15 per cent Lycra elastane fabric will not go transparent when wet.

▲ **St Trop:** one-piece swimsuit in navy and white from 80 per cent nylon and 20 per cent elastane.

▲ **St Trop:** navy and white swimsuit from
80 per cent nylon and 20 per cent elastane.

Ariella

◀ **Ariella:** one-piece swimsuit from
80 per cent polyamide and 20 per cent Lycra.
Photograph: Lycra only by DuPont.

▶ **Ariella:** one-piece swimsuit from
80 per cent polyamide and 20 per cent Lycra.
Photograph: Lycra only by DuPont.

▲ **Anita:** 'Marmara' orange one-piece maternity swimsuit with Lycra content.

▶ **Anita:** 'Nila 9501' one-piece maternity swimsuit with a large Lycra content.

▲ **Speedo:** 'S2000' one-piece swimsuit from a warp knitted polyester elastane fabric with high-filament polyester micro fibre yarns and finished with a thermal treatment.

▶ **Speedo:** 'P.B.T. Endurance' one-piece swimsuit from 45 per cent polyester and 55 per cent P.B.T., a polyester variant, giving superior recovering properties.

▲ **Diva:** white one-piece swimsuit from a nylon and spandex mixture.

◀ **Diva:** blue one-piece swimsuit with patterned overskirt from a nylon and spandex mixture.

▲ **Sea Folly:** black zip swimsuit from nylon/elastane.

▶ **Sea Folly:** red zip swimsuit from nylon/elastane.

▲ **Rasurel:** stripy one-piece swimsuit from a nylon/Lycra mixture.

◄ **Rasurel:** blue-and-white print one-piece swimsuit from a nylon/Lycra mixture.

◄ **Rösch:** one-piece swimsuit from 80 per cent
polyamide and 20 per cent Lycra.
Photograph: Lycra only by DuPont.

▶ **Rösch:** one-piece swimsuit from 80 per cent
polyamide and 20 per cent Lycra.
Photograph: Lycra only by DuPont.

▲ **Gottex:** 'Jingle' black-skirted one-piece swimsuit with soft clips and white button trim made from nylon with Lycra.

▶ **Gottex:** one-piece swimsuit from 80 per cent polyamide and 20 per cent Lycra. Photograph: Lycra only by DuPont.

▲ **Jantzen:** racer back tank styled one-piece swimsuits from 85 per cent nylon and 15 per cent Lycra.

▶ **Jantzen:** 'Keyhole Back Tank' one-piece swimsuit from 83 per cent nylon and 17 per cent Lycra.

Jantzen

◄ **Karl Lagerfeld:** one-piece halter neck swimsuit from 80 per cent polyamide and 20 per cent Lycra. Photograph: Lycra only by DuPont.

▶ **Sam de Teran:** black one-piece halter neck strap swimsuit with boy-short legs from 88 per cent nylon and 12 per cent Lycra. Photograph: Tim Green.

▲ **Triumph:** 'Sun Select' one-piece swimsuit from 85 per cent polyester and 15 per cent elastane. The fabric only allows the harmless UVA rays through to the skin, blocking out the harmful UVB rays almost entirely.

▶ **Triumph International:** one-piece swimsuit in Teflon-coated fabric. Teflon-coated textiles are water and dirt repellent. Teflon has no smell and barely changes the feel of the fabric which thus retains its original properties of air permeability, weight and drape.

▲ **Diva:** 1950s-styled white one-piece swimsuit from 80 per cent nylon and 20 per cent spandex.

▶ **Diva:** red-and-black one-piece swimsuit from a nylon and spandex mixture.

◀ **Raisins:** one-piece swimsuit made from 54 per cent cotton, 23 per cent nylon, 15 per cent acetate and 8 per cent elastane.

▶ **Pro Lines Leisurewear:** 'Madrigale' Fiji underwired swimsuit made from 80 per cent Lycra and 20 per cent cotton.

◀ **Maru:** 'Sun-Up' multi-coloured skooba swimsuit made from 80 per cent nylon and 20 per cent Lycra.

▲ **Ari:** one-piece swimsuit made from 80 per cent polyamide and 20 per cent Lycra. Photograph: Lycra only by DuPont.

▲ **Speedo:** 'Bodyshell' white high neck one-piece swimsuit. The 'Bodyshell' yarn cuts down on the rays of light that can pass through the swimsuit to the body.

Speedo

▲ **Rasurel:** one-piece swimsuit made from
a nylon and Lycra mix.

▲ **Patricia of Finland:** swimsuit with built-in underwired bra from polyamide Lycra.

▶ **Patricia of Finland:** swimsuit with built-in soft bra from polyamide Lycra.

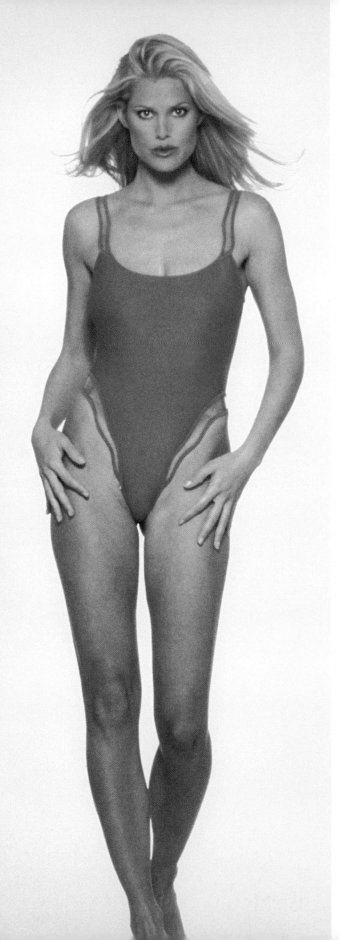

◄ **S/G by Gottex:** 'Jennifer' high-cut leg swimsuit with double strap and scalloped edging at the legs and plastic inset strips. Made from 80 per cent nylon and 20 per cent Lycra.

▶ **S/G by Gottex:** 'Blue Jeans' denim blue underwired one-piece swimsuit with multi-coloured floral trim. Made from 80 per cent nylon and 20 per cent Lycra.

◄ **Anita:** blue one-piece post-mastectomy swimsuit with goldfish pattern.

▲ **Beachcomber:** one-piece blue-and-white print swimsuit from 80 per cent polyamide and 20 per cent elastane.

◀ **Diva:** 'Hot 7086' patterned one-piece swimsuit from 80 per cent nylon and 20 per cent spandex.

▲ **Diva:** blue high neck underwired one-piece swimsuit from a nylon and spandex mixture.

▲ **Sunflair:** one-piece swimsuit from
44 per cent polyester, 44 per cent tactel,
8 per cent Lycra and 4 per cent polyamide.
Photograph: Lycra only by DuPont.

▶ **Bendigo:** 'Spaghetti Tank'. Rubber is
stretched and woven to create a fabric made
from 34 per cent polyurethane, 18 per cent
wool, 13 per cent nylon, 16 per cent nat
gummi and 19 per cent polyester.

The Two-Piece Swimsuit

The bikini is an abbreviated, minimal woman's two-piece swimsuit, consisting of a bra and brief. In its modern form, it was designed by Frenchman Louis Reard on the 30 June 1946. The style was simultaneously introduced by a better-known designer, Jacques Heim, who called it *Atome*. In the same year, the USA conducted its atomic bomb test on a Pacific island called Bikini Atoll. The suit was modelled by Micheline Bernardine, a nude dancer from Casino De Paris Revue Show, on 5 July 1946 and was immediately christened 'bikini' for its shock value and contemporary associations.

The bikini became highly popular in France immediately, but by the 1950s it had been adopted by the rest of the world, largely as a result of its exploitation by the film industry. Marilyn Monroe and Diana Dors promoted the bikini – and themselves – the latter appearing at the Venice Film Festival in 1955 wearing a 'mink' bikini (she later admitted it was made of rabbit). In the 1960s, Brigitte Bardot made the bikini her own and revolutionized the cinema's attitude to bare flesh. A string of beach movies were aimed at teenagers and the bikini was publicized further in movies such as *Bikini Beach* and *How to stuff a wild bikini*. Bikinis were seen on traditional seaside postcards, in the 'Carry On' movies, and on beauties such as Ursula Andress (*Dr No*) and Raquel Welch (*One Million Years B.C.*). A number of novelty suits were also produced, notably the nappy suit, a bikini made from white terry towelling.

Perhaps the most famous innovator in swimwear is designer Rudi Gernreich, who was responsible for the topless suit, a symbolic gesture of freedom in tune generally with attitudes of the period. Other designs of the time were the hip-rider suit, a two-piece swimsuit with low-slung pants or a skirt, showing the navel and the 'Gay 90s' suit (1960s), a two-piece, circular-striped, knitted suit with knee-length or hip-length short-sleeved top. The latter was much imitated in the jersey suits of the 1980s. By the late 1960s crochet bikinis, with only a few linking stitches at the side, could be seen and the popularity of the bikini was firmly established.

▶ **S/G by Gottex:** 'Zanzibar' black-and-white zebra print two-piece with an underwired bra and shorts from nylon with Lycra.

In the 1970s the bikini was increasingly featured in sophisticated glamour photography as fashion designers and photographers alike began to include it in their work.. Girls in bikinis were seen promoting fast cars and motorbikes. Further diminishing in size in the mid-1970s, it encountered a feminist backlash. 'Mini-bikinis' appeared and one psychologist is reported to have said that it was a way of disguising the shyness of those women who lacked confidence in everything but their physical attributes.

An example of such a style was the string bikini, which consisted of two minuscule triangles of fabric, held together by ties at either hip, whilst the top was attached by ties around the neck and back.

In the 1980s saw the introduction of the G-string bikini, contrasted by the 'power' swimsuit. Holiday-makers flocked to popular holiday resorts in warm climates, and sun-worshippers wore topless bikinis (or even sunbathed nude, though this can hardly be classified as 'swimwear'). The increasing brevity of the bikini was demonstrated by the thong, the 'rikini' and the loop. Another style was the blouson suit, which consisted of one or two pieces, a bloused effect which came below the natural waistline, the top having a built-in bra. This style was originally fashionable during the 1960s but was revived during the 1980s. Briefers, worn by men and boys, were very short trunks, similar to and inspired by bikini pants, and were made from elastic or knitted fabrics. The improvised scarf suit was developed in response to badly-designed swimsuits. Women tied scarves around their bosoms for tops, and wore cut-off jeans for bottoms, creating individual outfits.

The bikinis of the 1990s are sleek and sexy, baring bottoms with styles like the tanga bikini, a design revolution popularized by supermodels such as Naomi Campbell. Designer bikinis have been shown by Gianni Versace, Katharine Hamnett and Ralph Lauren. Vivienne Westwood has also confirmed that less can mean more; Karl Lagerfeld designed a sensational micro-bikini for the House of Chanel in 1995.

▶ **Diva:** 1950s-style two-piece with halter neck top and boy-shorts from 80 per cent nylon and 20 per cent spandex.

◀ **SG by Gottex:** bikini and matching mini skirt.

▶ **Speedo:** 'Sonic' top from a nylon/Lycra mixture and a jacquard waistband short from 100 per cent nylon.

◀ **Jantzen:** underwired bikini from 85 per cent nylon and 15 per cent Lycra.

▶ **Jantzen:** underwired two-piece from 47 per cent polyester, 33 per cent nylon and 14 per cent Lycra.

Jantzen

▲ **Sunflair:** two-piece from 80 per cent polyamide and 20 per cent Lycra. Photograph: Lycra only by DuPont.

▶ **Opera:** bikini and sun dress from 78 per cent acetate, 15 per cent polyamide and 7 per cent Lycra. Photograph: Lycra only by DuPont.

◀ **Bendigo:** cire mock continuous
underwire top with 'Rio' pant from
80 per cent nylon and 20 per cent Lycra.

▲ **Bendigo:** black lace classic with 'Rio'
pant from 80 per cent polyester and
20 per cent Lycra.

▲ **Rasurel:** blue patterned two-piece.　　　▶ **Beachlife:** bikinis with Lycra.

Beachlife

◄ **St Trop:** spotted turquoise two-piece from
80 per cent nylon and 20 per cent elastane.

▶ **St Trop:** royal blue patterned two-piece
from 80 per cent nylon and 20 per cent elastane.

◀ **Slix:** 'Orange Blossom' two-piece with a
halter neck top and skirted bottoms from a
polyester and Lycra mixture.

▶ **Slix:** two-piece with shorts made from 45
per cent cotton, 45 per cent polyester and
10 per cent Lycra.

▲ **Sea Folly:** yellow string bikini from nylon and elastane.

▶ **Sea Folly:** navy-and-white short set from polyester/cotton/elastane.

▶ **Diva:** patterned two-piece swimsuit with thin double strapped top and flyaway shorts with side pocket. Made from a nylon and spandex mixture.

◀ **Diva:** 'Trixie 7179' black-and-white suit from 72 per cent nylon and 28 per cent spandex.

Gottex: 'Desire' black-and-white polka dot bikini with white daisy trim. Triangle bra cups and tiny brief from nylon with Lycra.

S/G by Gottex: 'Marlen' pink halter neck top with boy leg briefs shown with matching fitted blouse. Made from 80 per cent nylon and 20 per cent Lycra; blouse in mesh effect Lycra.

Gottex

▲ **Jantzen:** underwired two-piece made from 69 per cent nylon, 20 per cent polyester and 11 per cent Lycra.

▶ **Jantzen:** triangle bikini made from 85 per cent nylon and 15 per cent Lycra.

◀ **Bendigo:** metallic push-up underwired top with thong pant from 78 per cent polyester and 22 per cent Lycra.

▲ **Bendigo:** 'Ombre' two-piece bikini made with 18 per cent Lycra.

◀ **Sea Folly:** black halter neck short set from nylon/elastane, seen with navy-and-white stripe swimsuit from polyester/cotton/elastane and a nylon lining.

▲ **Sea Folly:** black short set from nylon and elastane seen with black-and-white dot swimsuit from polyester/cotton/nylon and elastane.

▲ **Raisins:** 'Daisy and Me' power pad lime
green patterned underwired two-piece with
high-cut legs; made from 100 per cent Lycra.

▲ **Raisins:** blue-and-white patterned
two-piece made from 89 per cent cotton
and 11 per cent Lycra.

▲ **Slix:** 1977 white two-piece string bikini made from 100 per cent nylon.

▶ **Slix:** 'Jasmine' two-piece made from 88 per cent nylon and 12 per cent Lycra, worn with pareo made from 100 per cent nylon.

▲ **Diva:** black-and-white polka dot bikini top with halter neck straps and black high-cut leg bottoms made from 72 per cent nylon and 28 per cent spandex.

▶ **Diva:** yellow T-shirt over two-piece bikini.

◀ **St Trop:** royal blue two-piece from 80 per cent nylon and 20 per cent elastane.

▲ **Anita:** 'Janet' black-and-white striped two-piece from the 'Beach Secret' range made with a large Lycra content.

◀ **Triumph International:** two-piece
swimsuit made from 85 per cent polyamide and
15 per cent Lycra.
Photograph: Lycra only by DuPont.

▶ **Rasurel:** two-piece made from a nylon
and Lycra mix.

Cover-Ups

Wraps — sarongs, pareos, shirts, skirts and even trousers — are increasing on offer, making both the swimsuit and bikini more versatile than ever, especially given the extra support to the bust that is now possible with developments in swimwear.

A T-shirt is probably the most fundamental item for mixing and matching with separates. A sheer shirt is a good cover-up, and can be worn as an evening jacket when accompanied by a camisole, bustier or bodysuit. It can also be knotted under the bust for a 1940s' look.

Sarongs are available as long or short wraps which can be tied around the waist or hips, on top of a bikini or swimsuit. Tied at the bust or at an angle under the arms they give a long-line look.

Loose skirts, such as the wrap-over style, can be worn over most bikinis and swimsuits and can also be paired with a cotton T-shirt, knotted blouse or cropped top.

Loose palazzos are an alternative to the sarong for those who prefer trousers. They are especially flattering for the fuller figure. Full-length cotton trousers in a lightweight fabric that will absorb moisture, such as cotton, might be an alternative, particularly in warmer climates.

Walking shorts can be teamed with a bikini top and a jacket for cooler weather. Drawstring shorts, which are usually loose and less fitted than walking shorts, are another option; these are knee length or slightly longer.

Sun dresses should be kept loose so that they can be slipped easily over beachwear or swimwear. Button front styles are very versatile as they can be worn as a jacket over other items. Halter necks or thin spaghetti straps set far apart on the shoulders are flattering and can take a T-shirt underneath on cooler days.

▶ **Triumph International:** underwired bikini with seamed cup and high cut leg brief from 80 per cent polyamide and 20 per cent Lycra elastane. The skirt is in polyester chiffon and has a side tie.

▲ **Slix:** 'Simply Textures' one-piece halter neck made from 100 per cent polyester with a white wrap from 90 per cent nylon and 10 per cent Lycra.

▶ **Slix:** 'Pot Pourri' bandeau one-piece swimsuit and black sarong. Swimsuit from 80 per cent nylon and 20 per cent Lycra; sarong from 100 per cent polyster georgette.

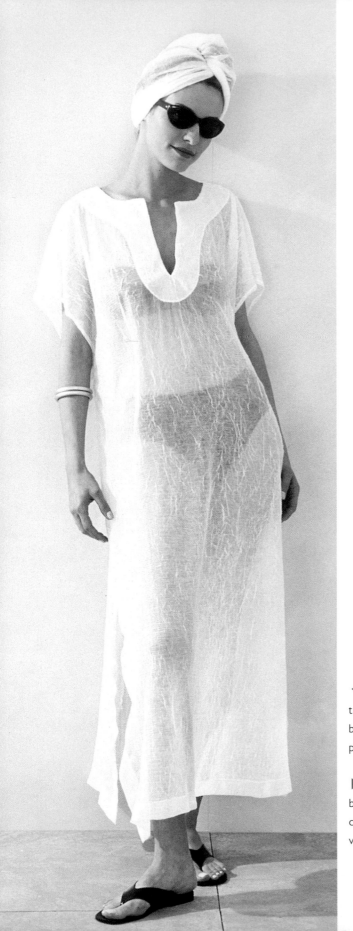

◀ **Diva:** cream and white kaftan with turban from 100 per cent polyester over a black bikini from 80 per cent nylon and 20 per cent Lycra.

▶ **Gottex:** 'Exquisite' turquoise floral bikini from 80 per cent nylon and 20 per cent Lycra with 'Eternity' blouse from viscose georgette.

◀ **Jantzen:** 'Sumatra' high neck one-piece swimsuit from 80 per cent nylon and 20 per cent Lycra.

▲ **Diva:** sheer white shirt over a one-piece swimsuit.

Accessories

There is a multitude of headwear to choose from, ranging from turbans to wide-brimmed hats. A Captain's hat is crisp and white, and is decorated with gold braid, stars or a crest. This nautical style seems to be in fashion every season. A bandanna, simply a scarf tied around the head, also keeps you cool.

Wide-brimmed hats are usually made from straw. They can be angular and crisp, floppy or turned-up. A Panama is a practical hat which folds up, and is good at keeping the sun off sensitive skin. Baseball caps present a young and fashionable appearance. Similarly a visor gives a sporty look, but is essentially only a sun shield. Sunglasses are essential daytime beachwear.

Goggles are important for competitive swimmers, those who wear contact lenses or those with sun-sensitive eyes. The most important feature of goggles is a watertight seal. The only way to be sure the goggles seal correctly is to try them on. Gently press the goggles against your eyes to test for suction. If the goggles stick to your face momentarily, you have a good fit. The goggle strap holds the goggles in place. Red rings around the eyes indicate that the strap is too tight. If you find that you have to tighten the strap in order for the goggles to be watertight, a different style may be better. Replacement straps are available in an assortment of sizes and styles.

Sneakers and boat shoes are a practical choice for comfort and make good walking shoes. There is now a much wider choice of styles than previously, as the distinction between swimwear and casual sports wear blurs.

▶ **Sunflair:** two-piece swimsuit made from 80 per cent polyamide and 20 per cent Lycra. Photograph: Lycra only by DuPont.

▲**Jantzen:** 'Proswim' shoes.

◄**Jantzen:** swimming caps.　　　▲**Jantzen:** 'Sportline' shoes.

Index

Anita 36, 37, 111

Arena 13, 26

Ari 66

Ariella 24, 24

Arzuaga, Amaya 19

'Atome' 74

bandeau styles 3, 117

Beachcomber 69

Beachlife 87

Bendigo 73, 84, 85, 100, 101

bloomer suit 24

Borg, Björn 14

boy-leg shorts 10, 27, 53

CAD 10

cap 124

Chanel 22

chlorine resistant properties 14, 16, 26

competitive swimming 6, 8, 16, 22

corsetry 6 10, 22, 56

de Teran, Sam 53

Diva 40, 41, 56, 57, 70, 71, 77, 94, 95, 108, 109, 118, 121

Dors, Diana 74

drag reducing properties 24

drying properties 18, 22

dyeing 8, 18

exercise 6, 22

film 74

Fürstenberg 8

G-string 76

Gernreich, Rudi 74

goggles 122

Gottex 3, 48, 49, 66, 67, 75, 78, 96, 97, 119

halterneck styles 12, 22, 52, 53, 97, 108, 116

hats 122

Heim, Jacques 74

high-leg styles 10

Howell, Margaret 25

Huit 11

Jantzen 22, 26, 50, 51, 80, 81, 98, 99, 120, 124, 125

kaftans 118